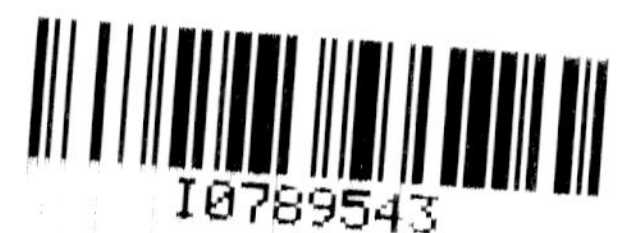

Amazing
Kangaroo Coloring Book

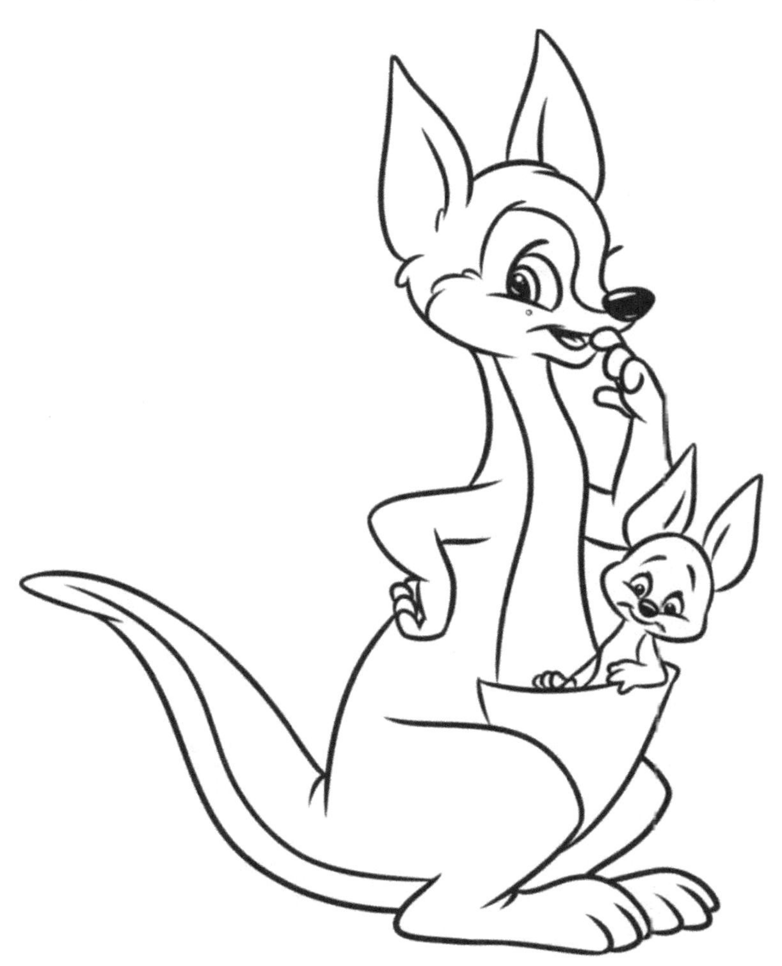

This Book Belongs ...To...

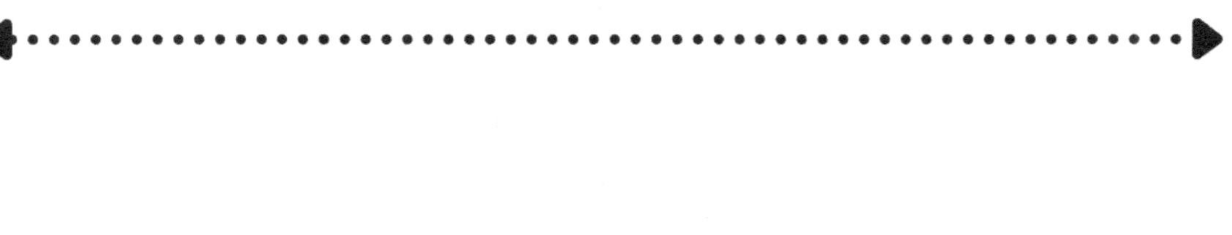

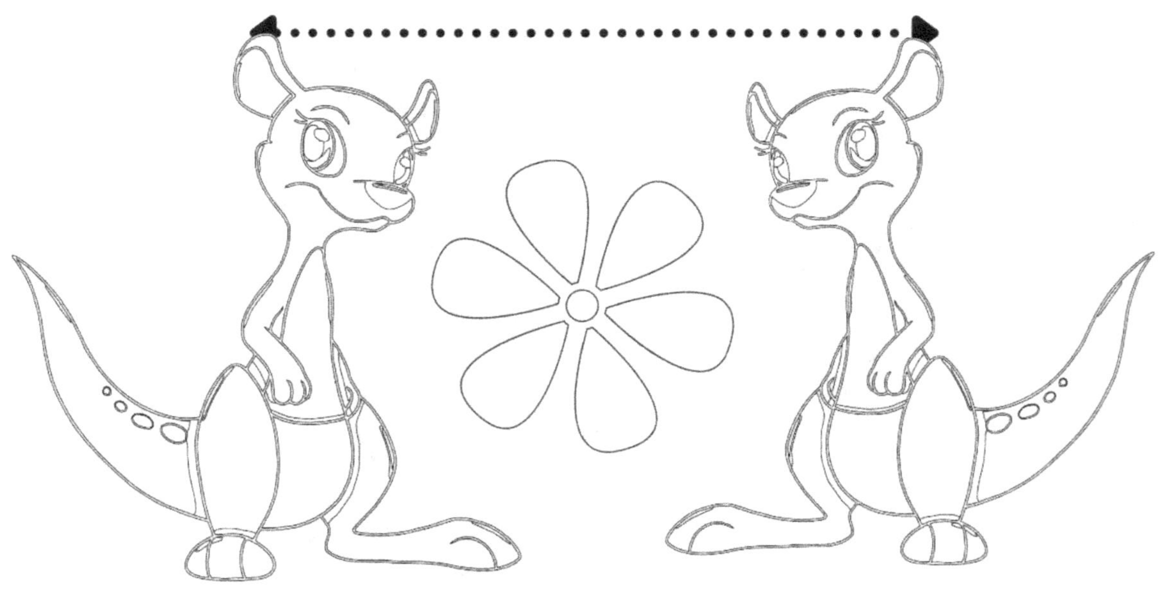

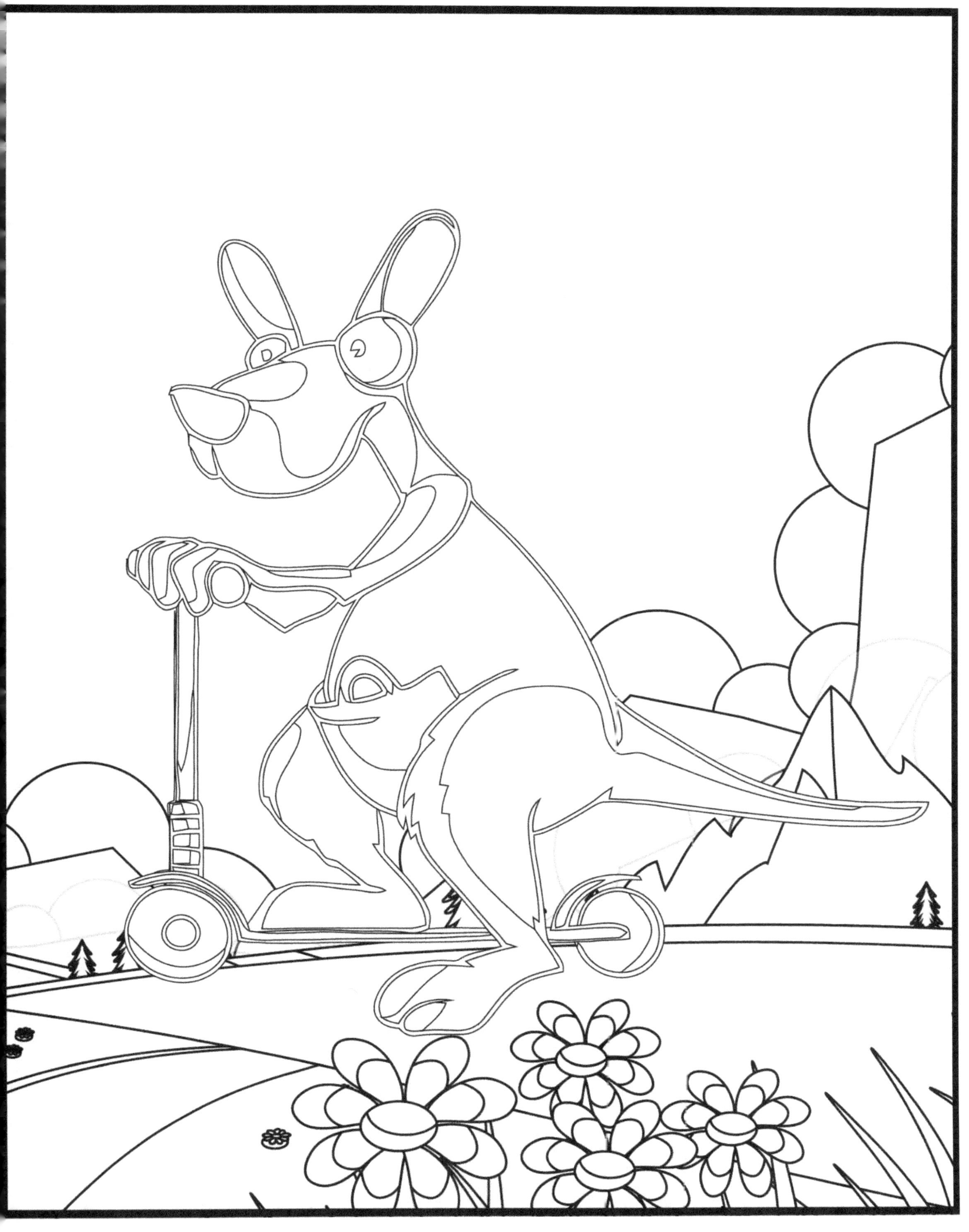

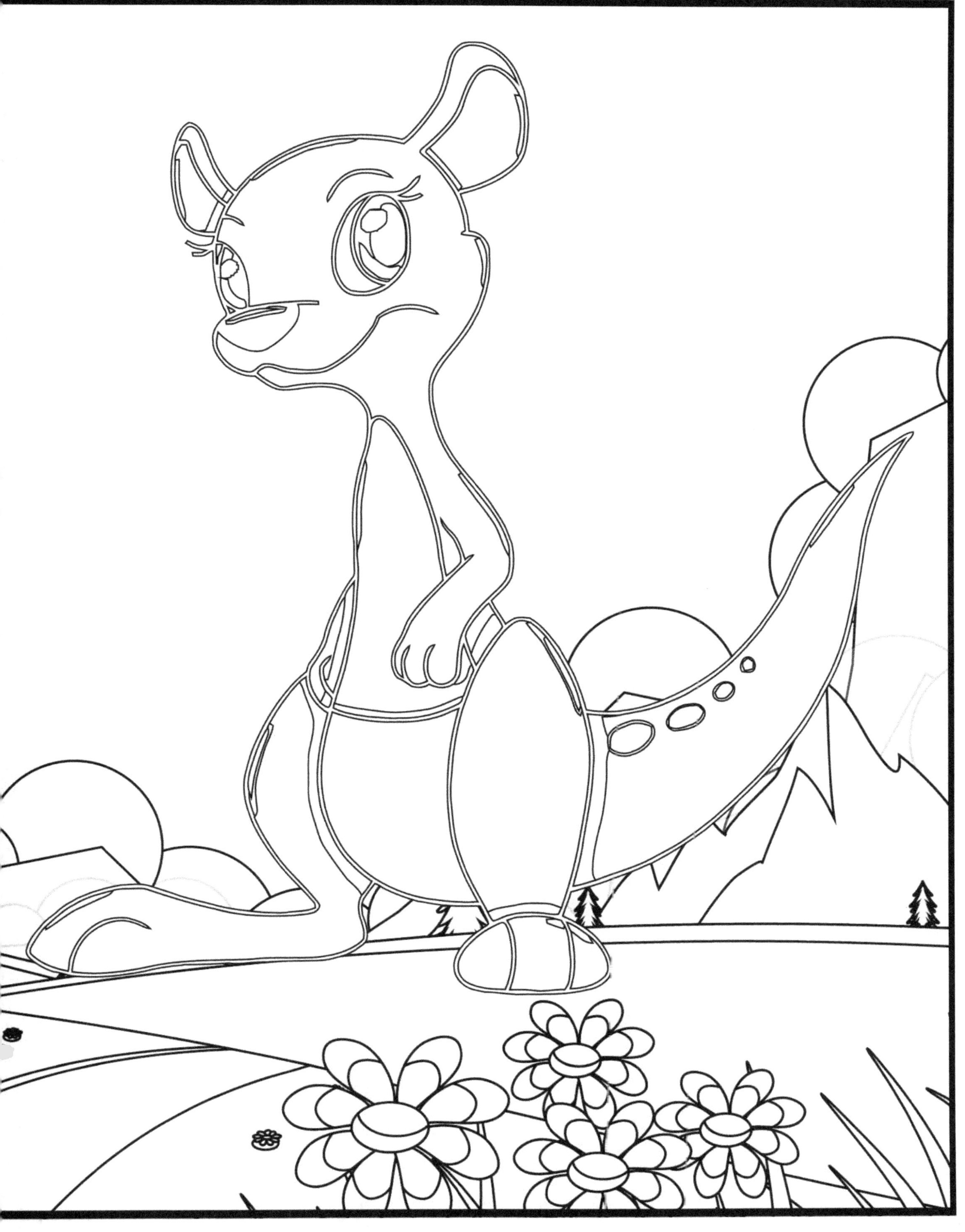

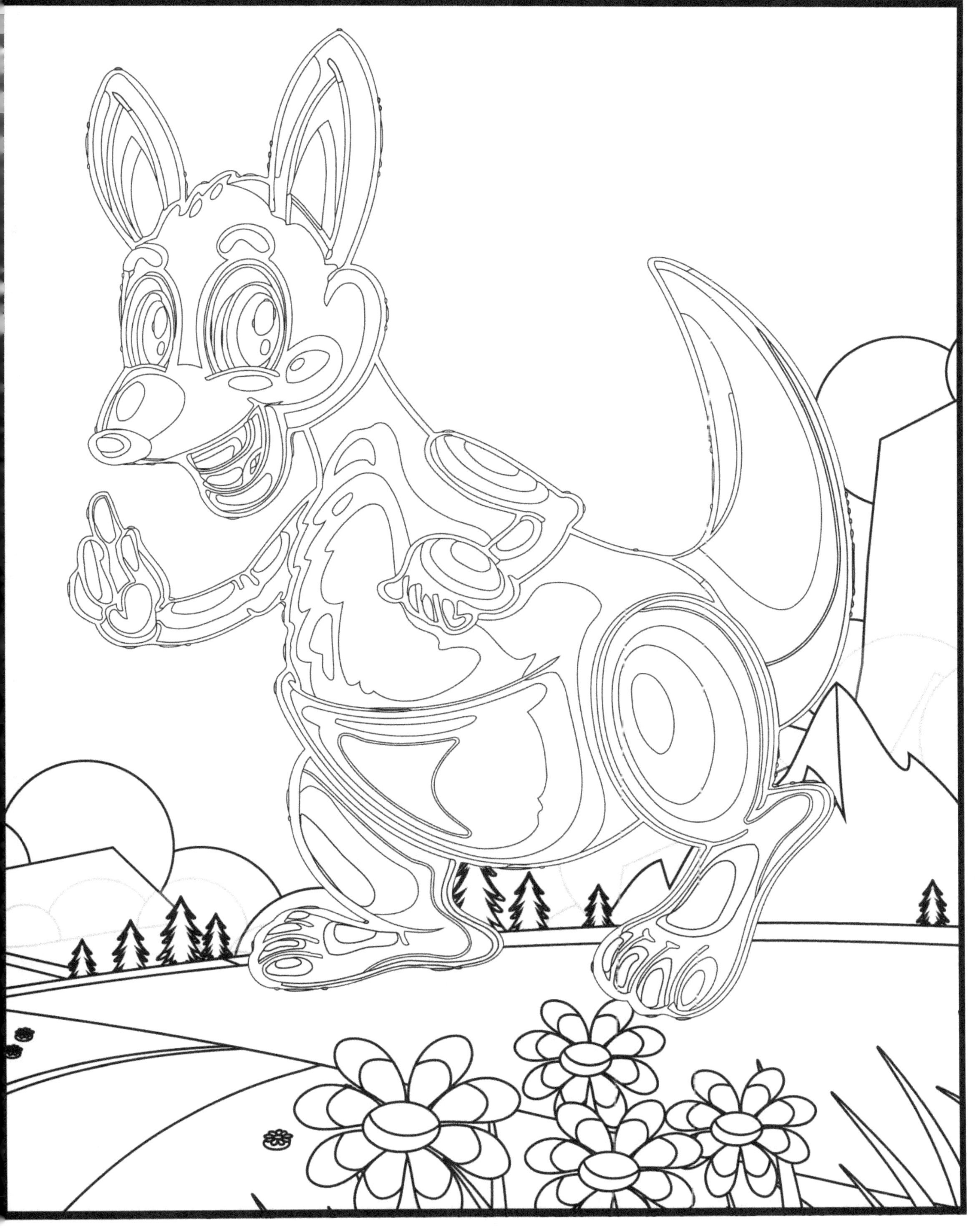

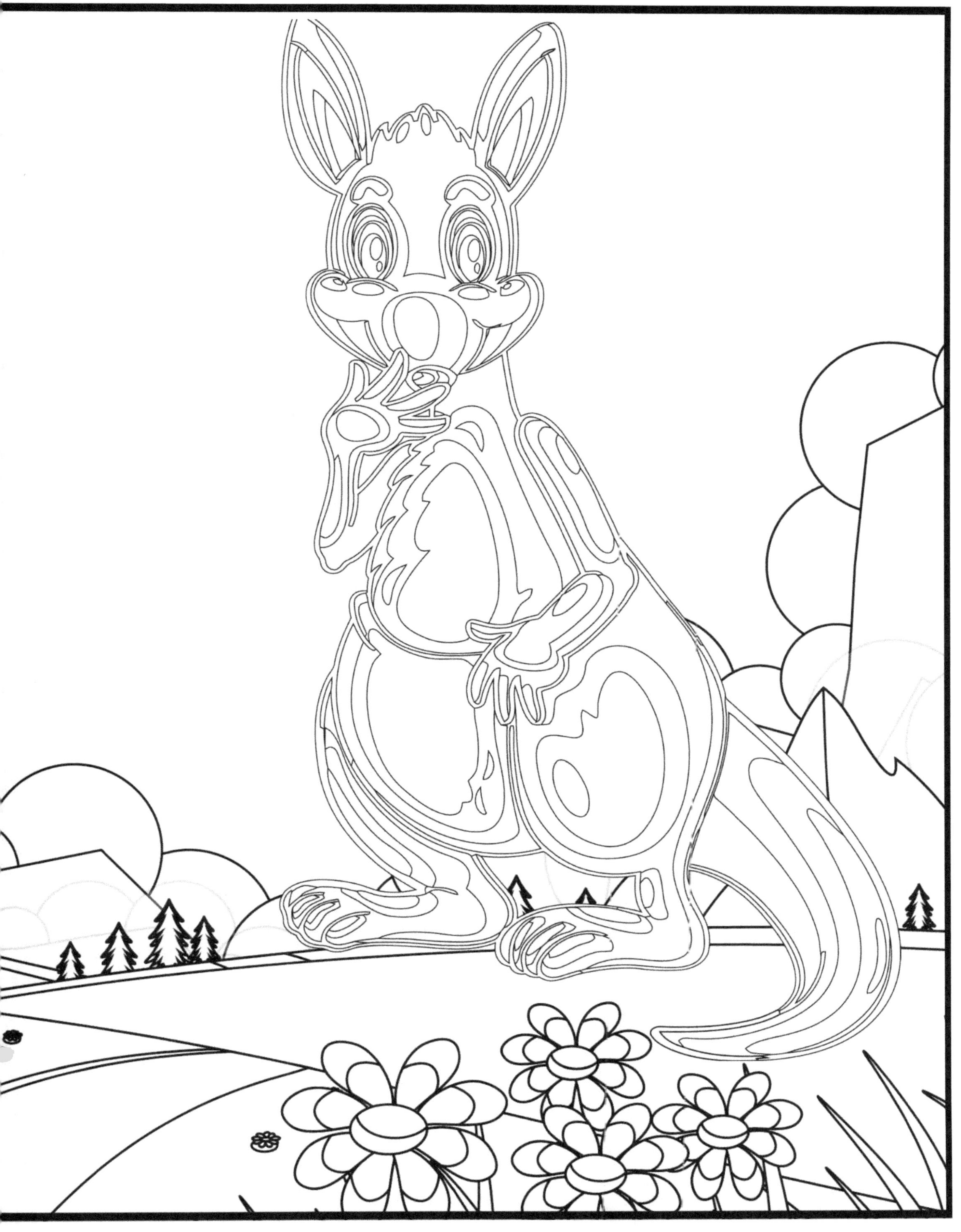

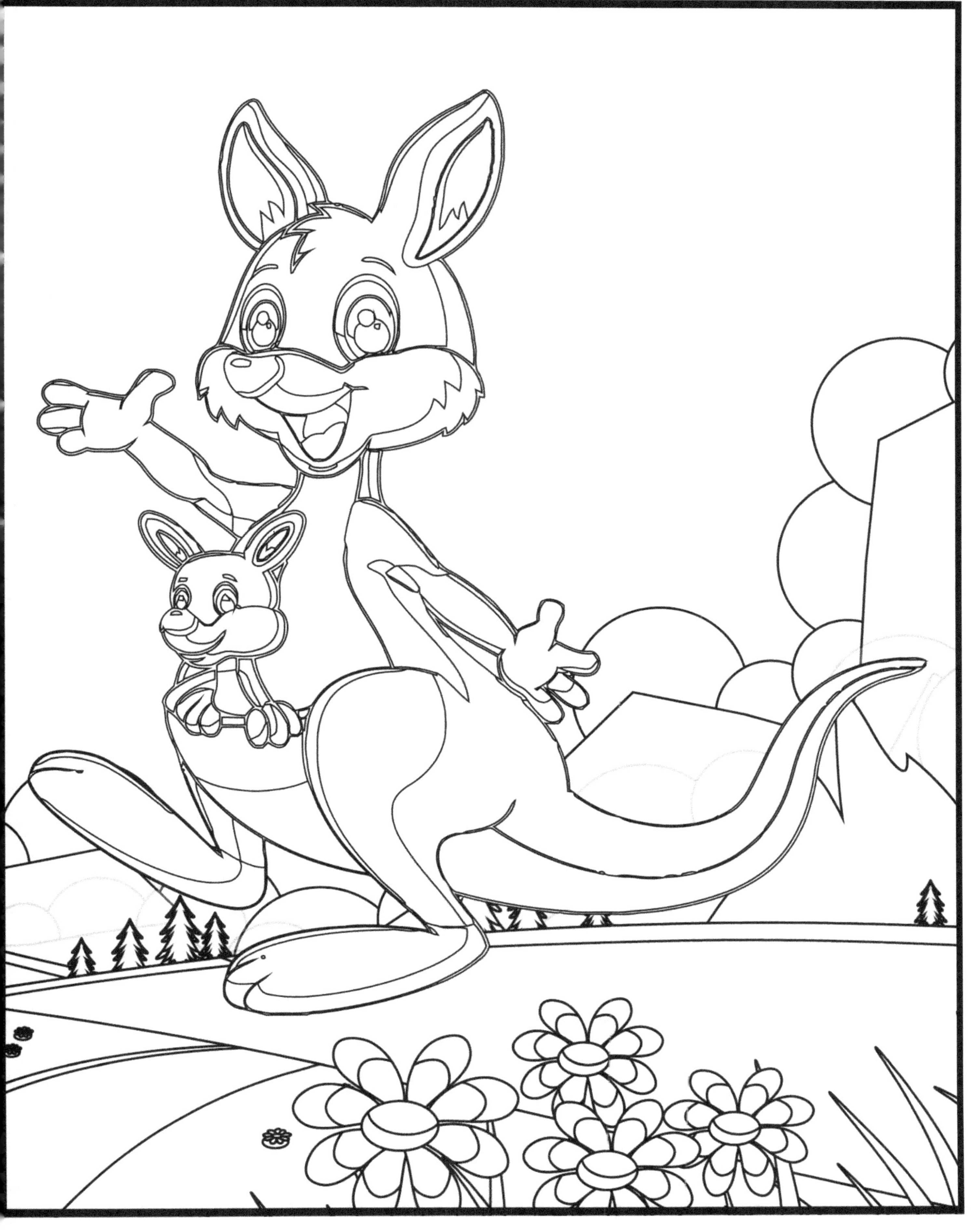

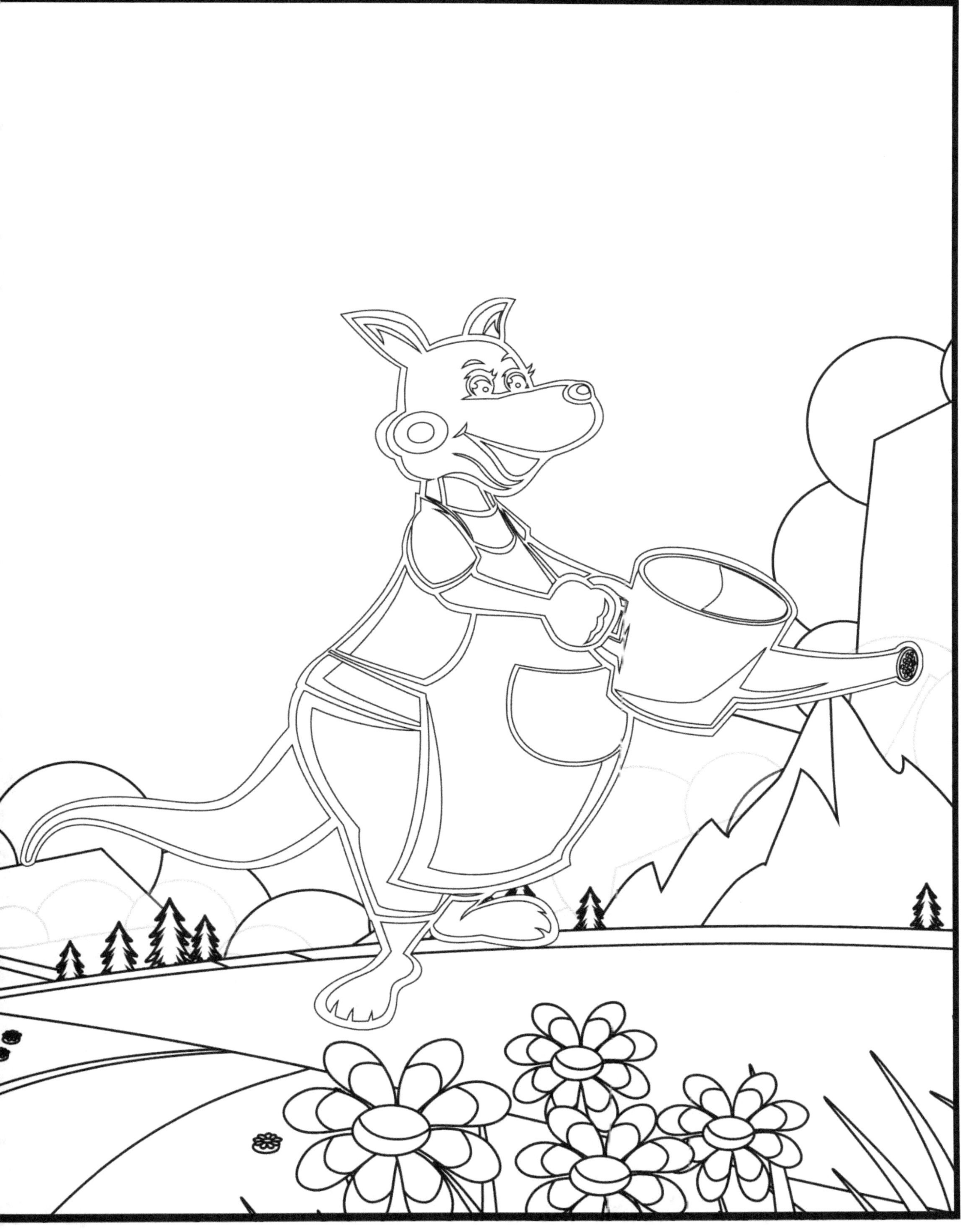

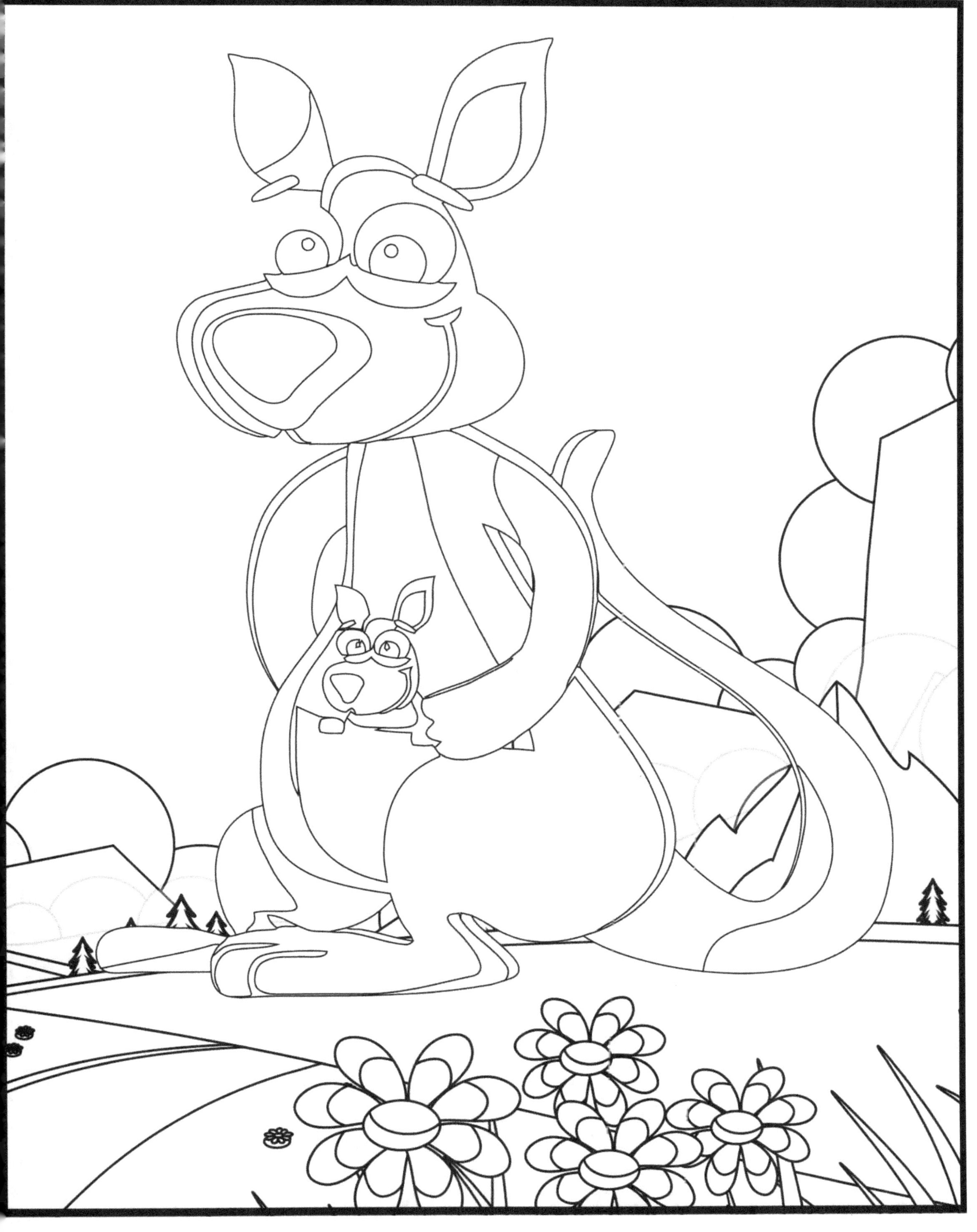

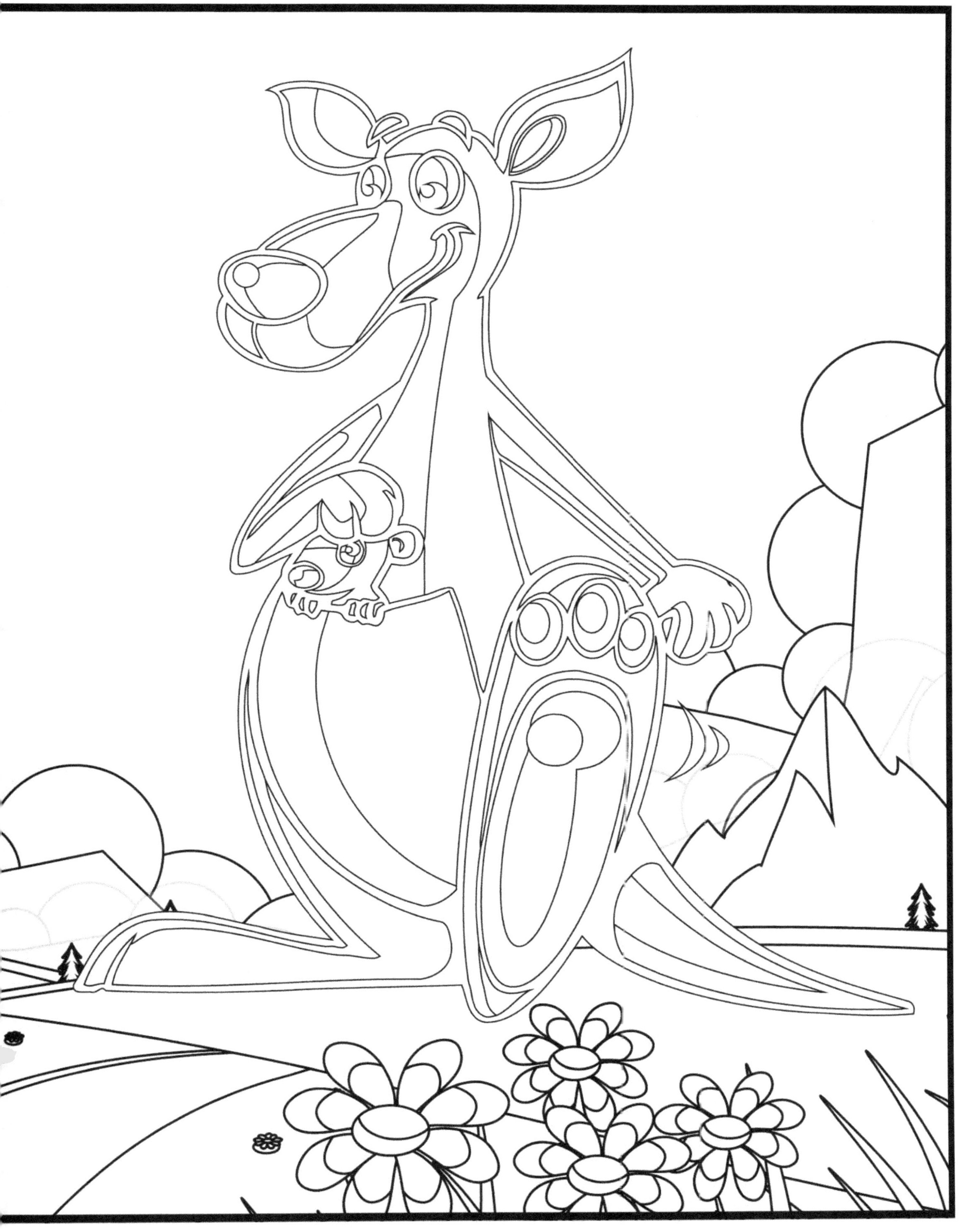

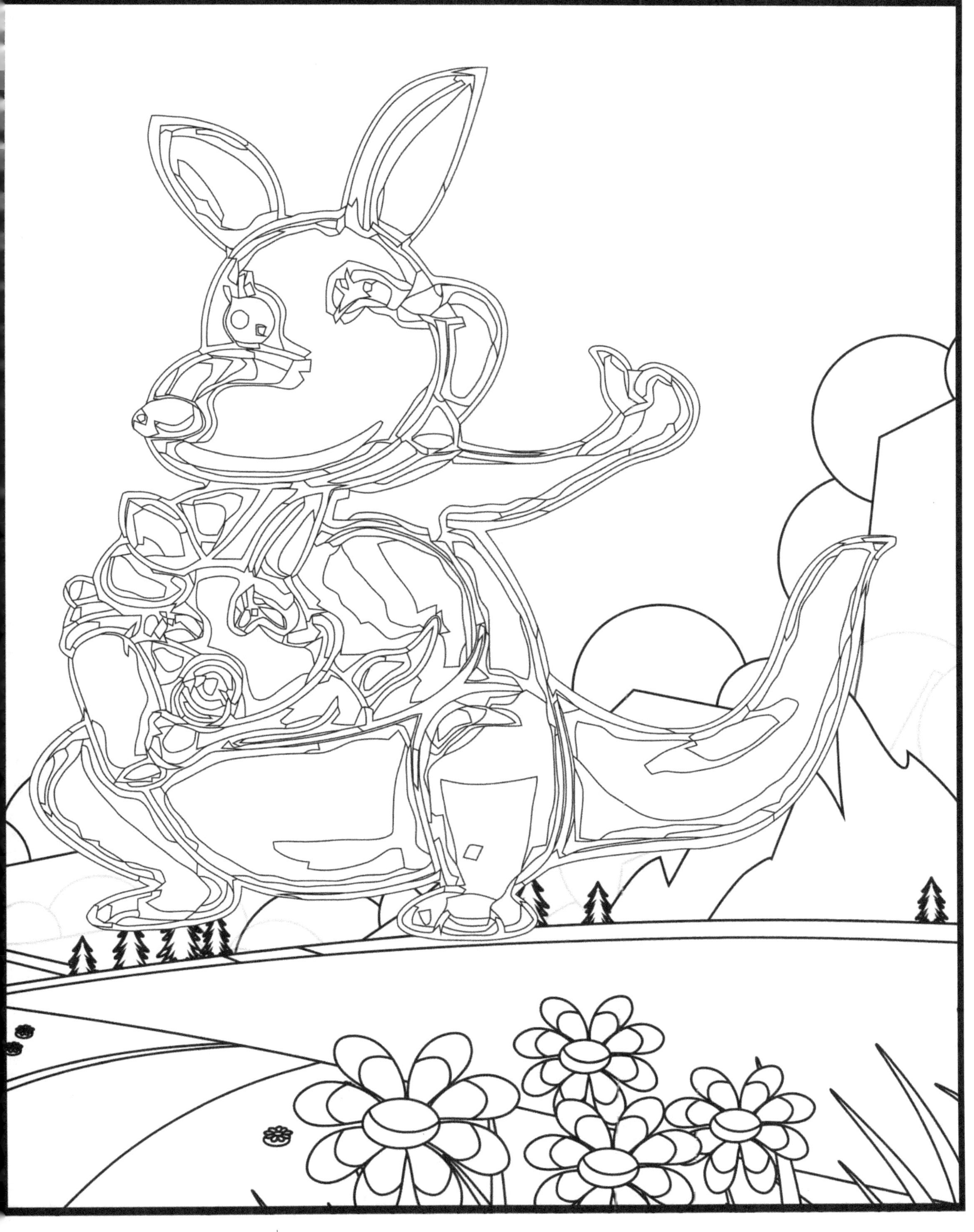

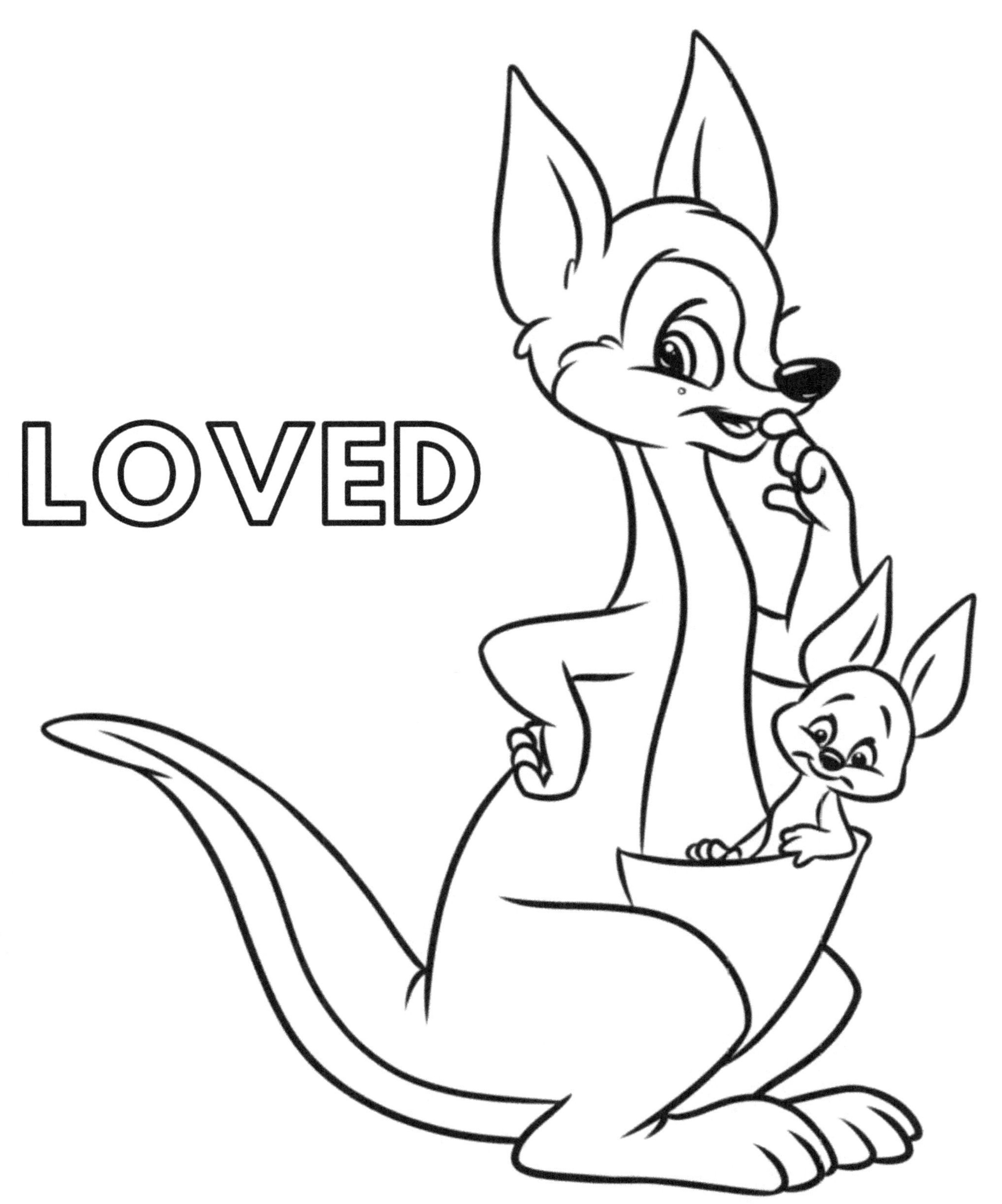
LOVED

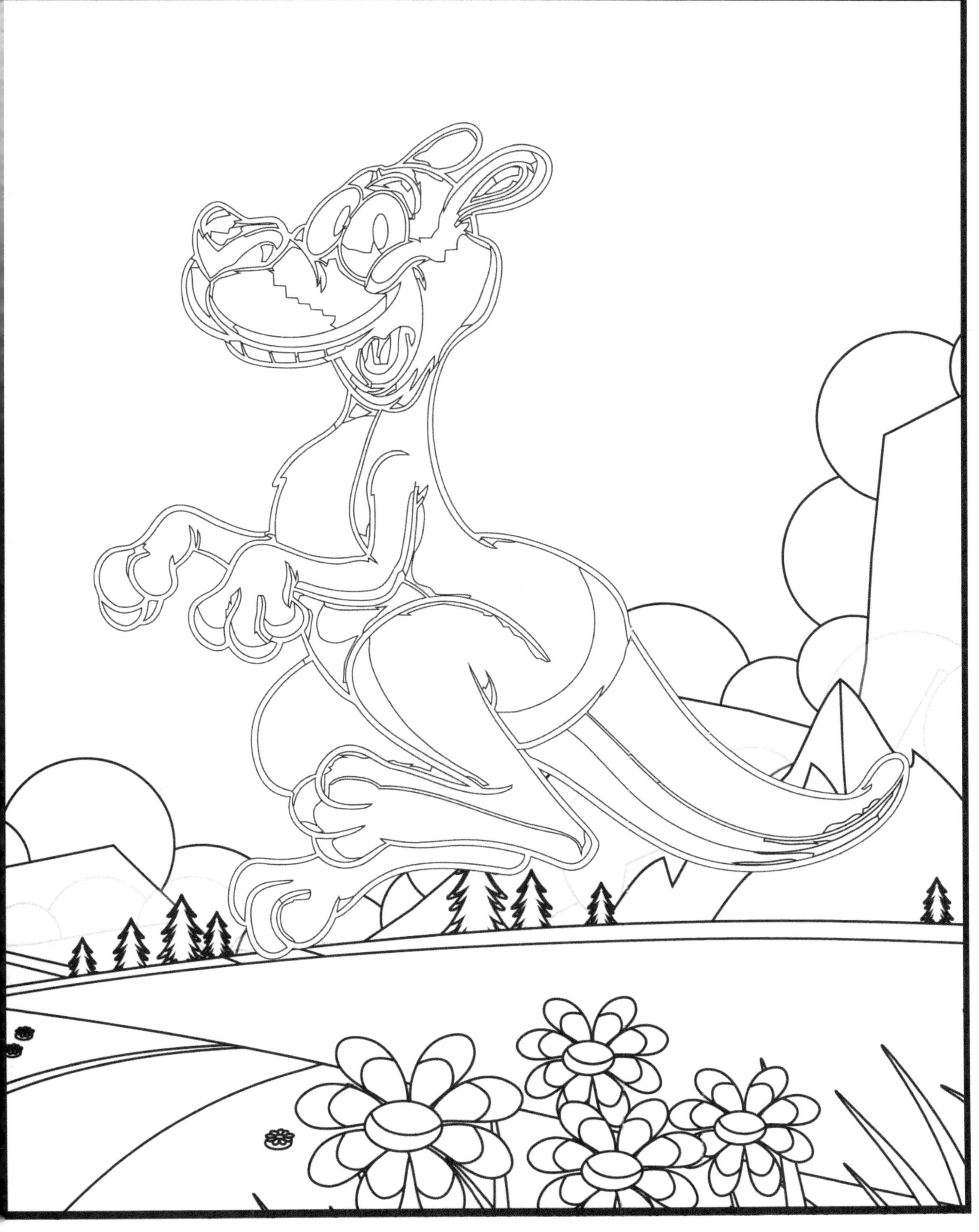

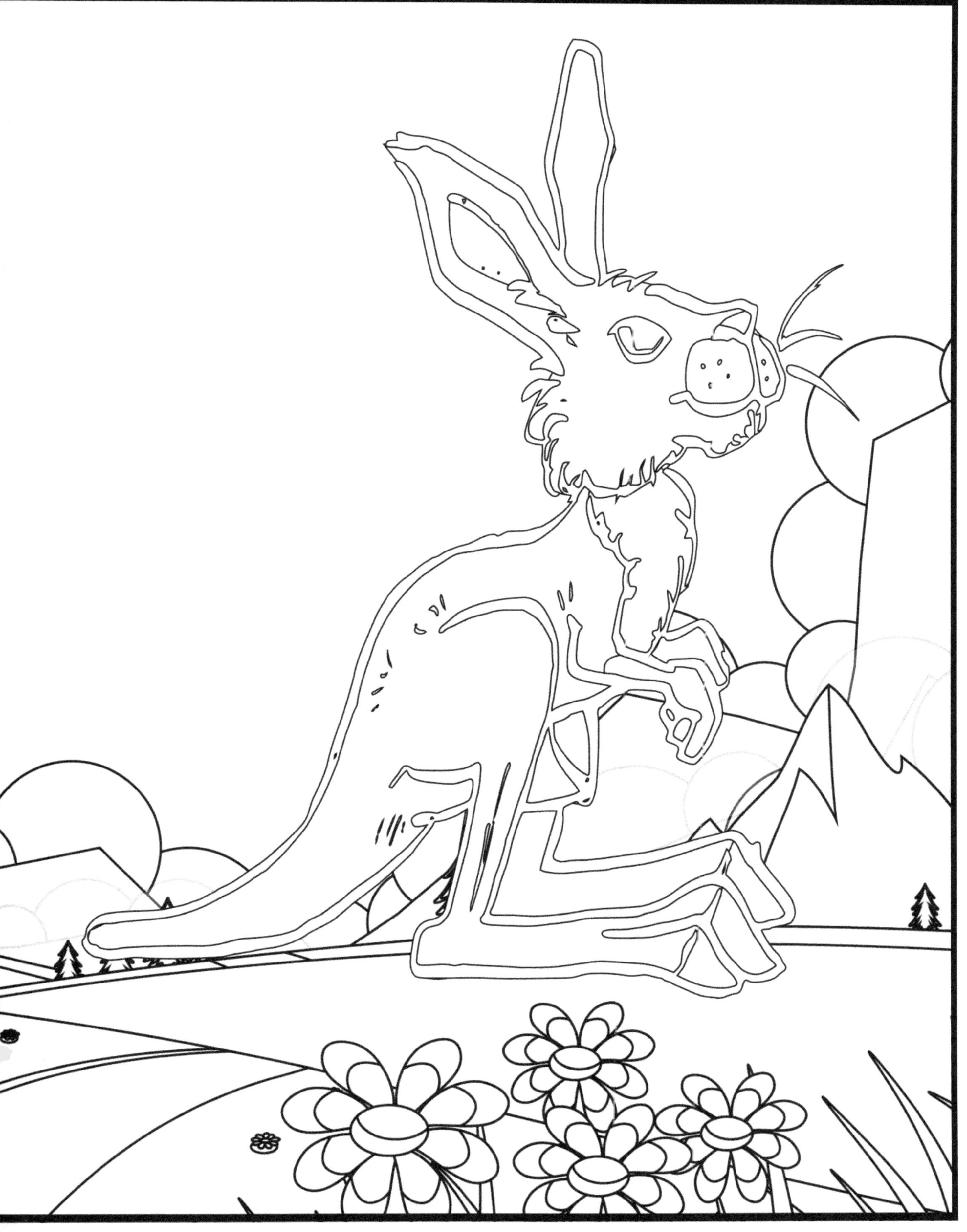

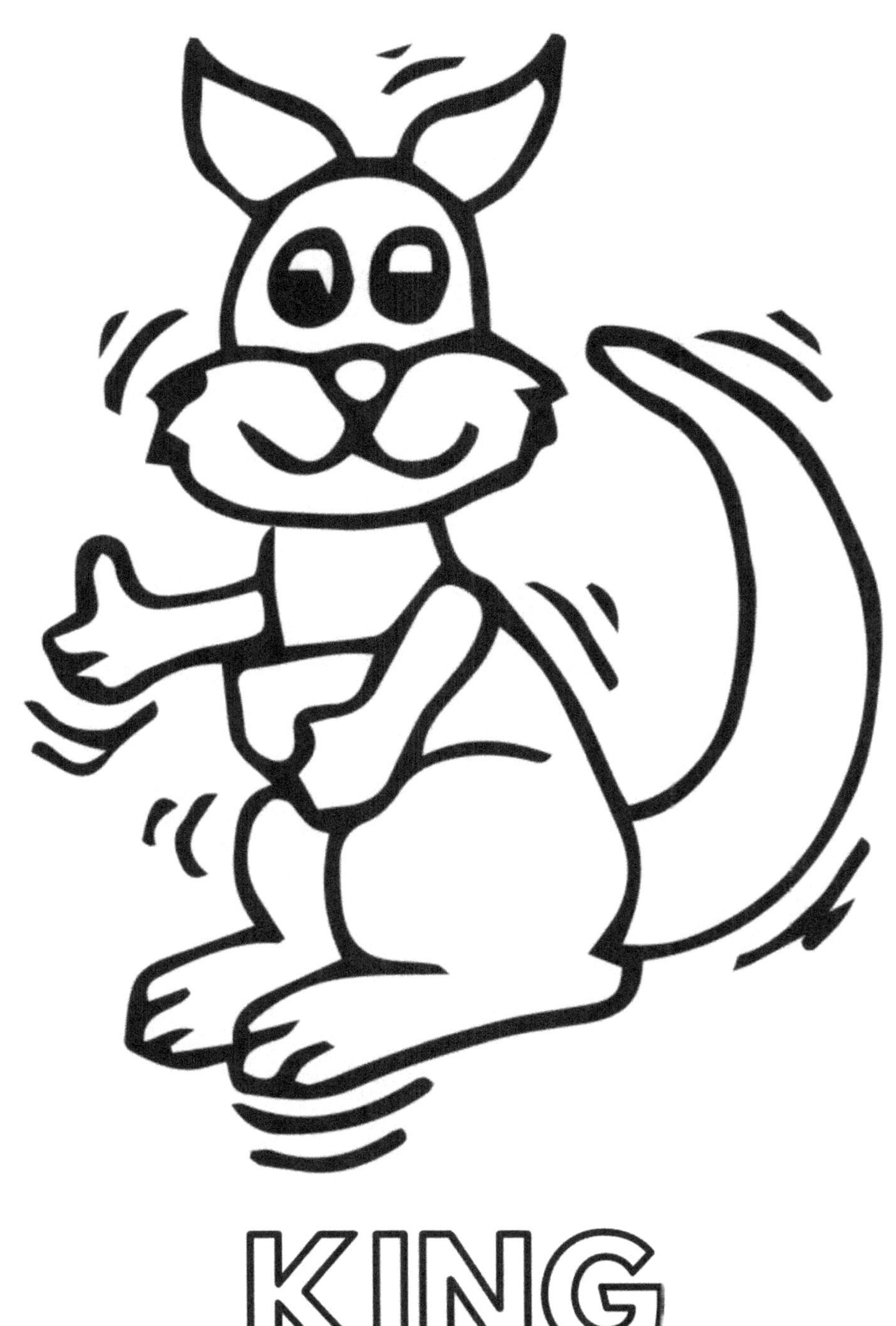

KING

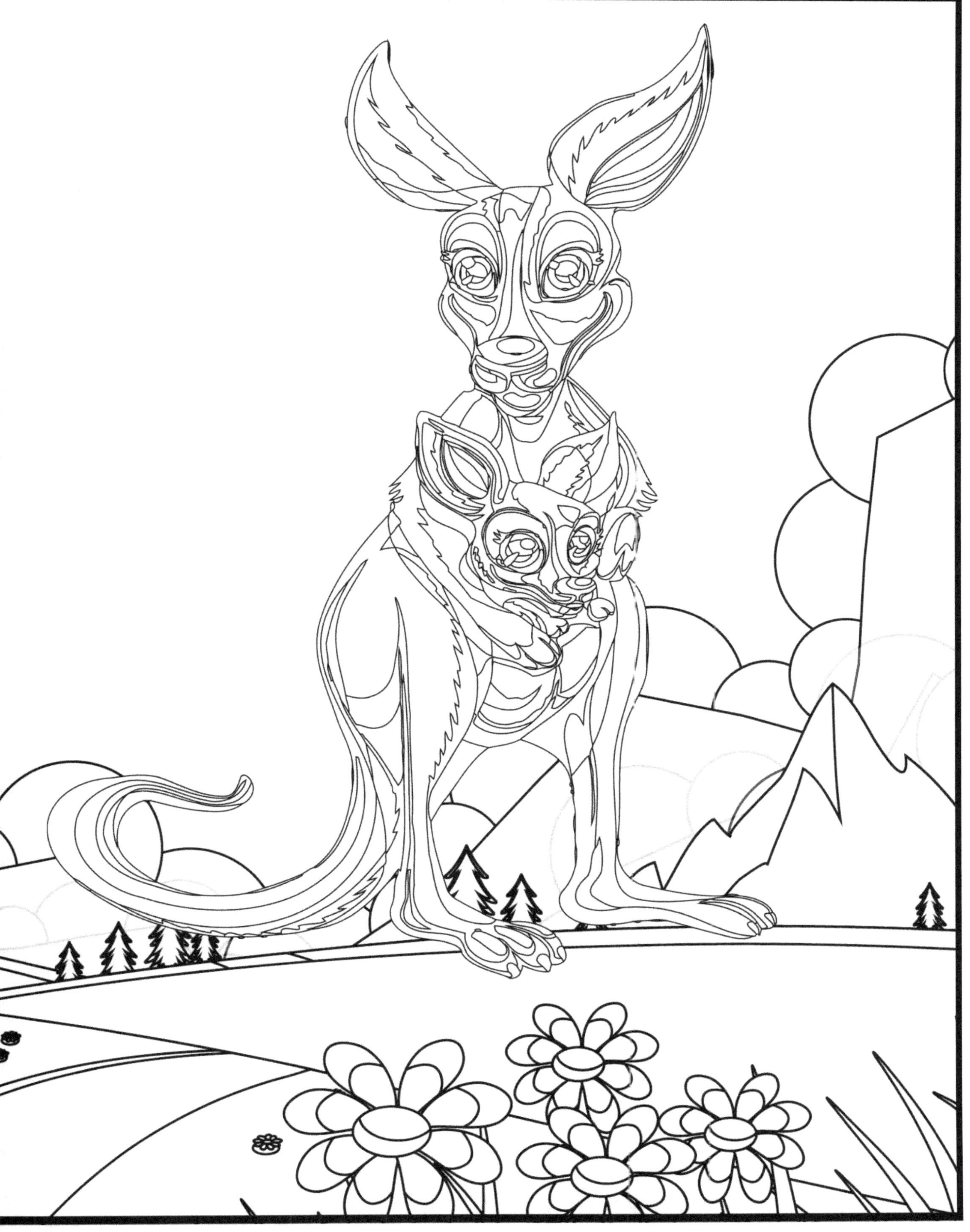

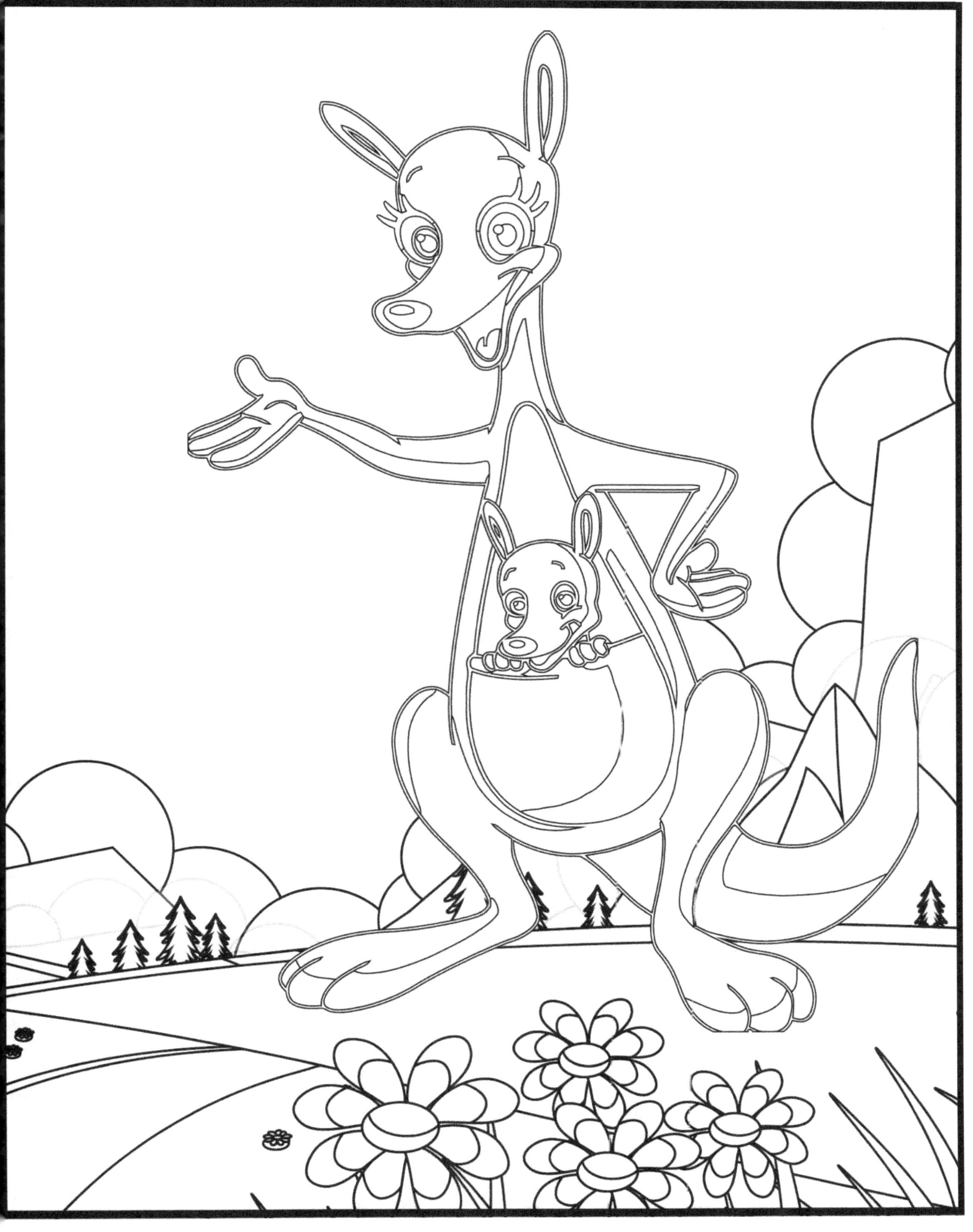

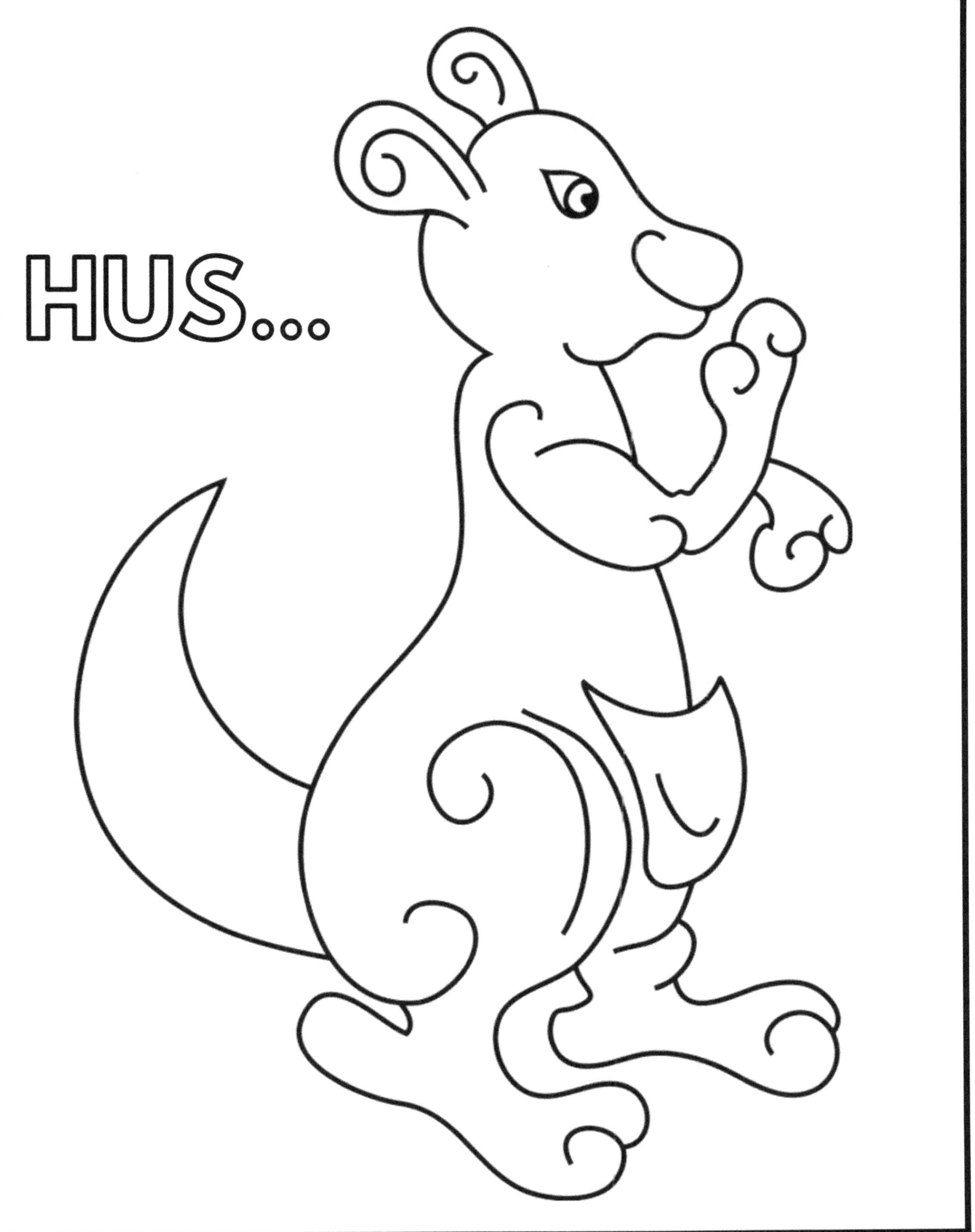

HUS...

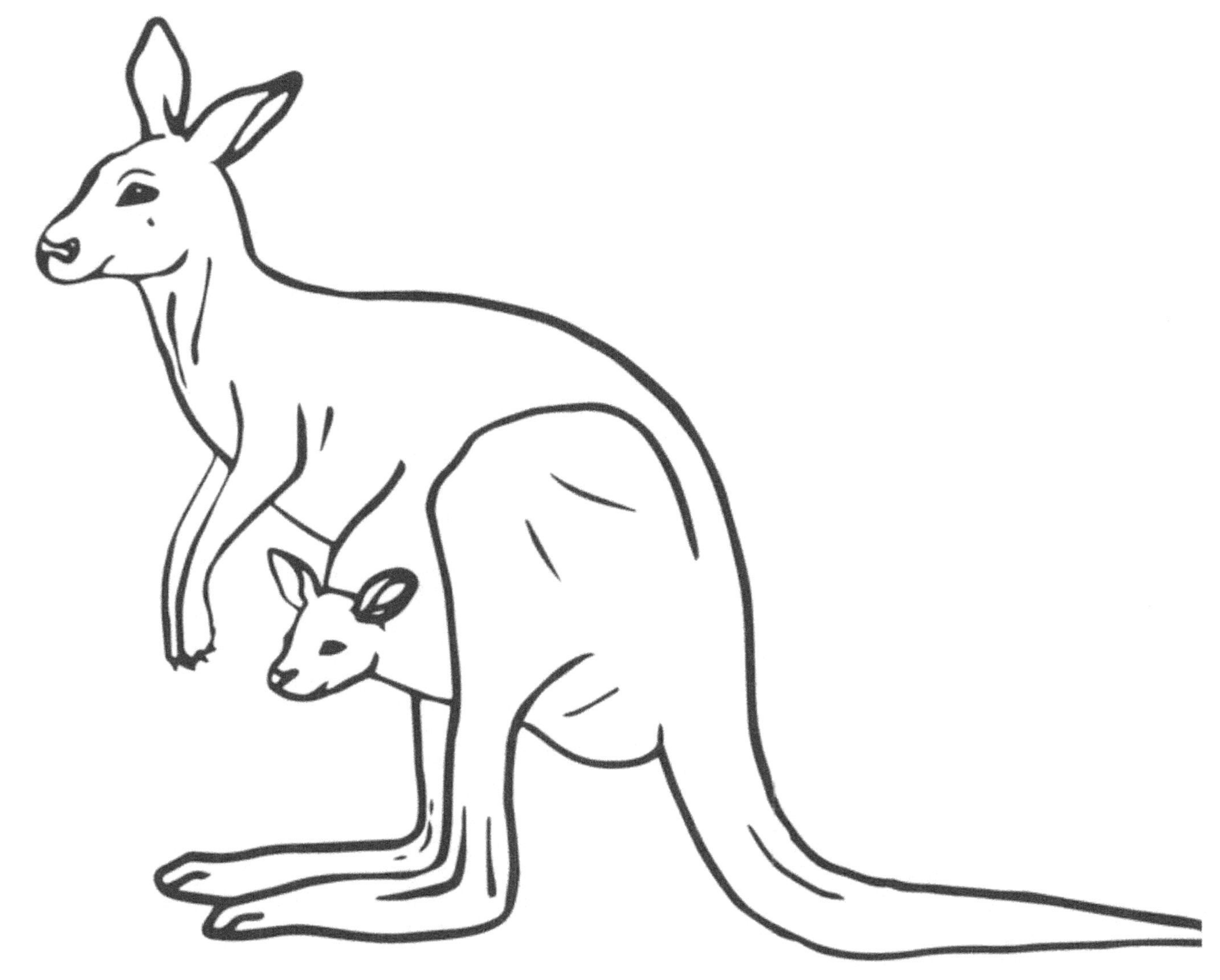

MOTHER KANGAROO

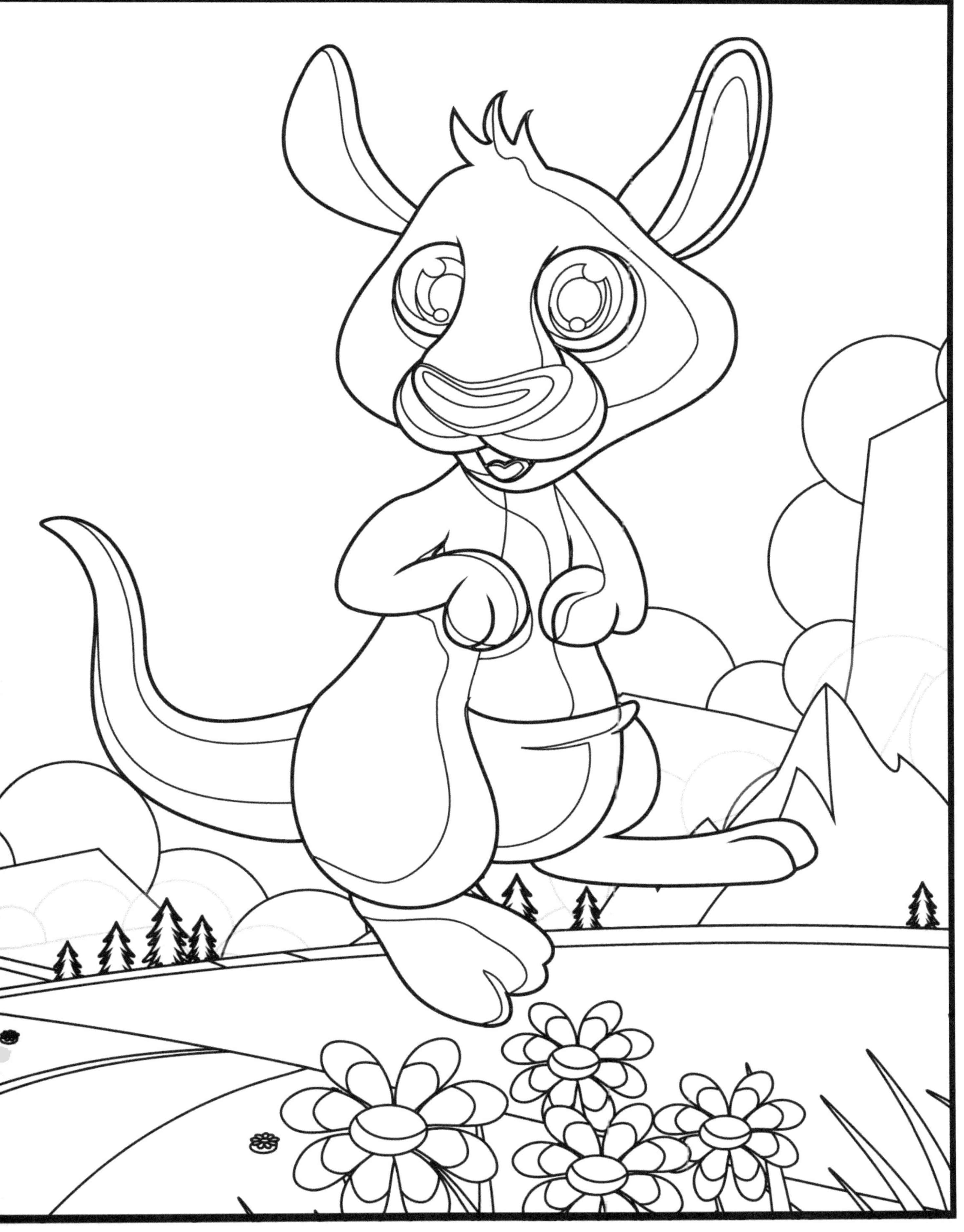

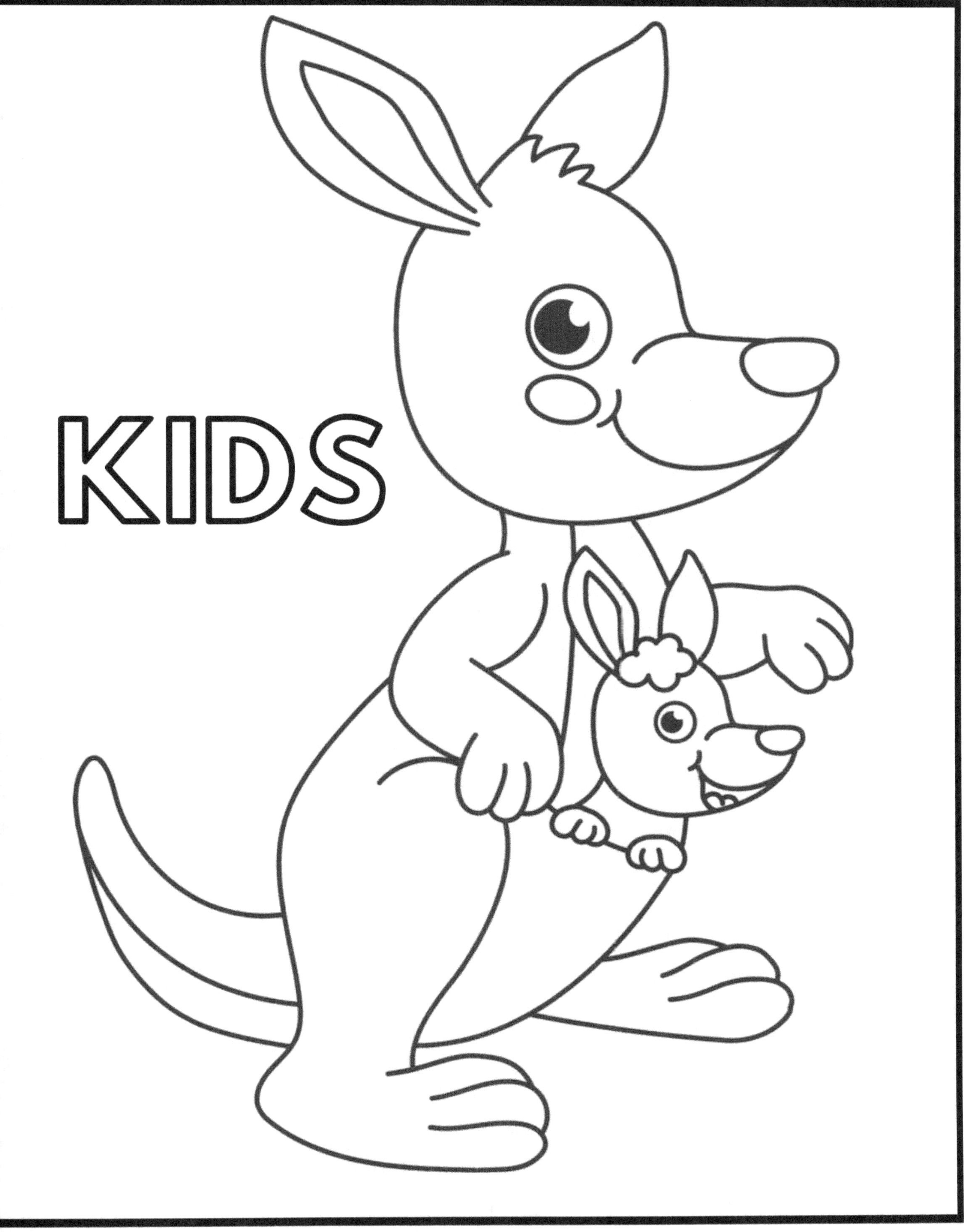

KIDS

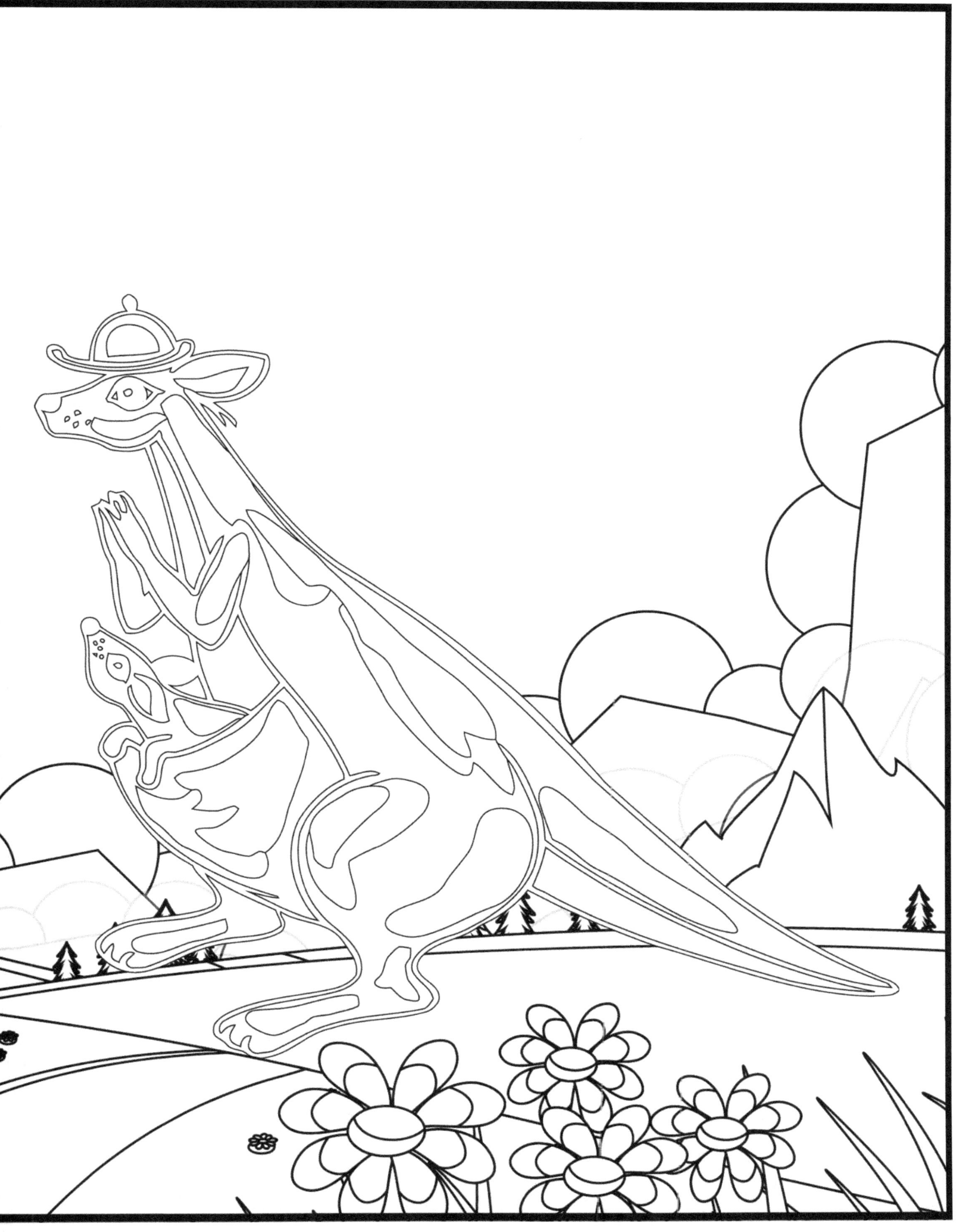

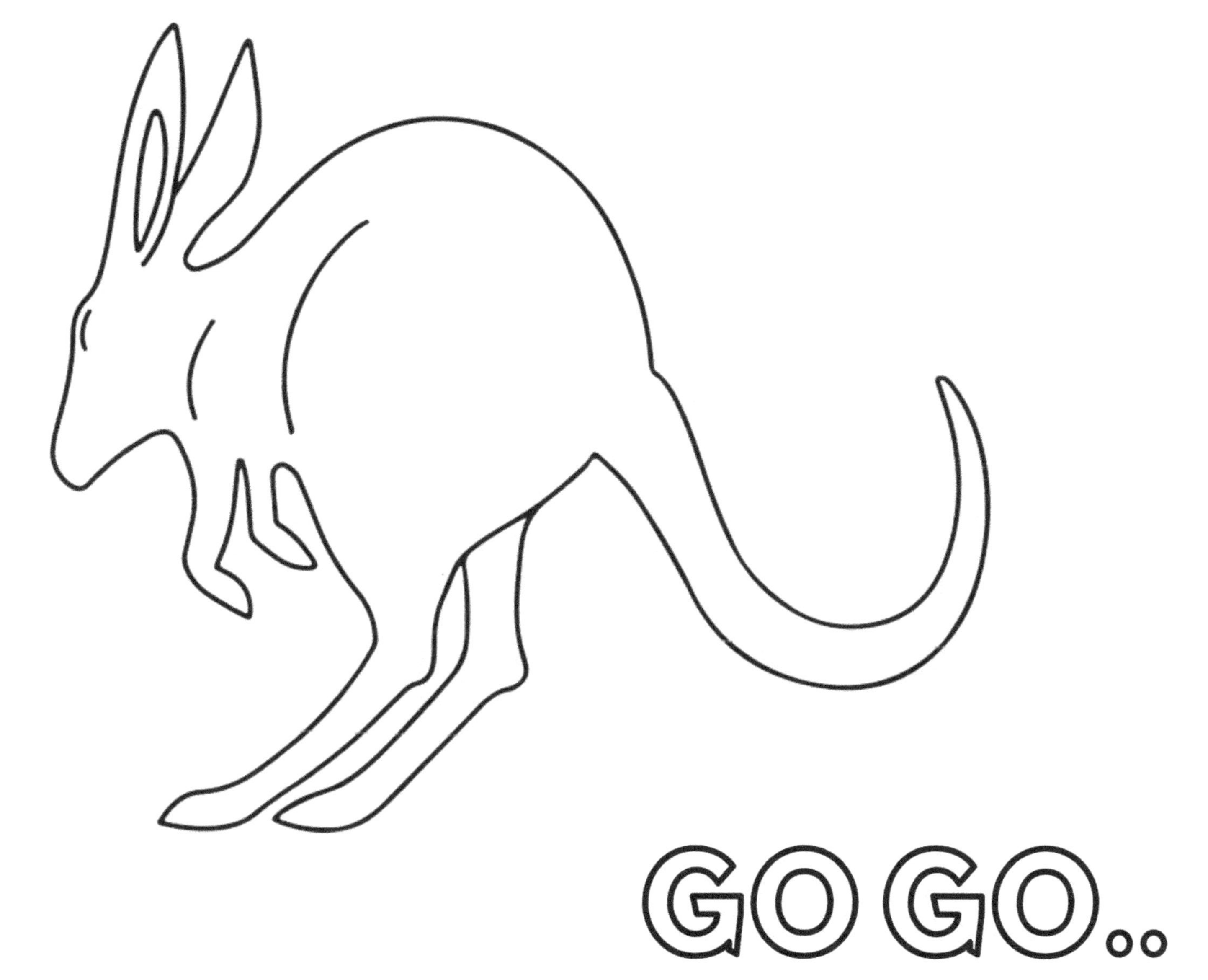
GO GO..

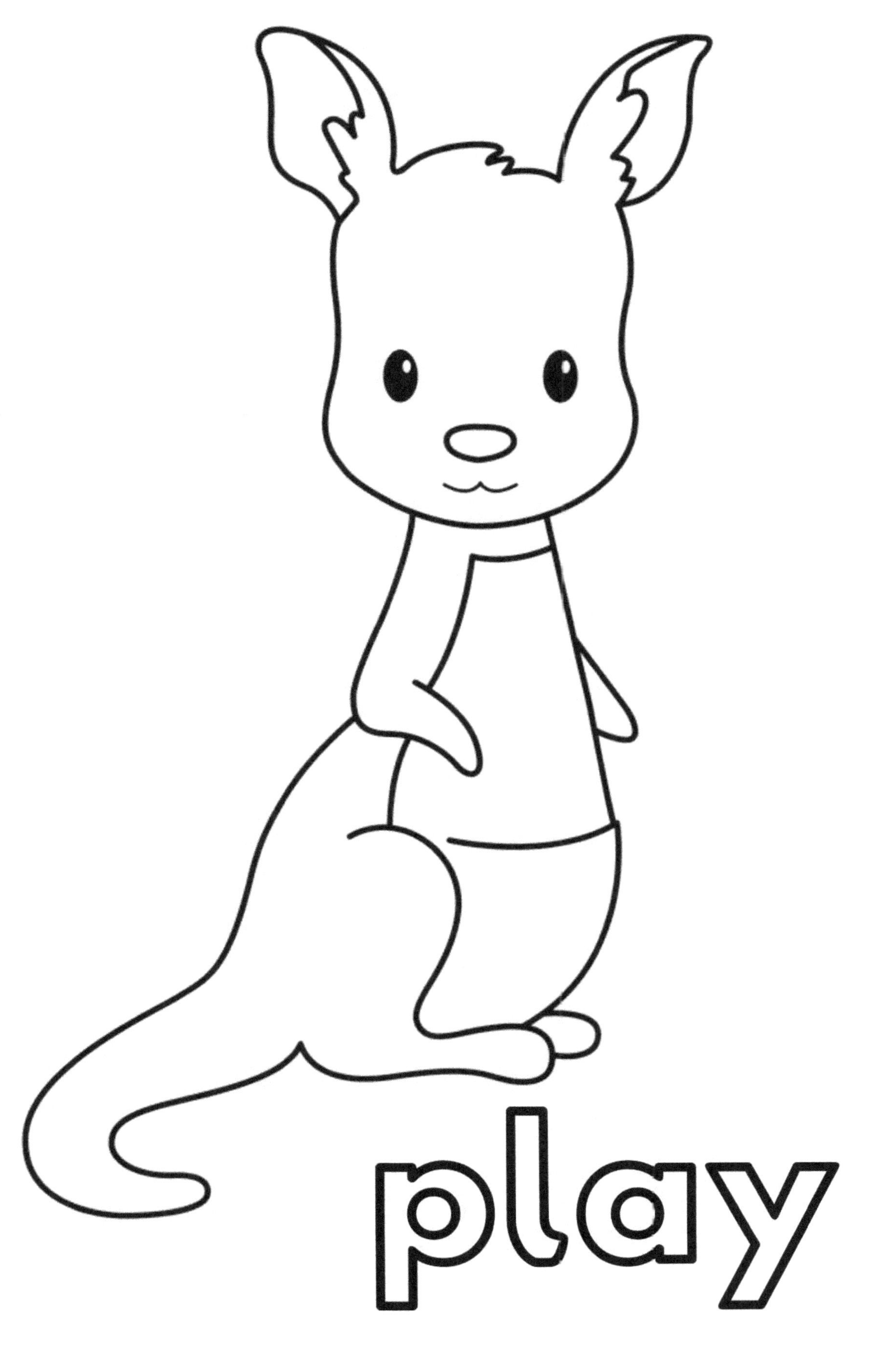

play

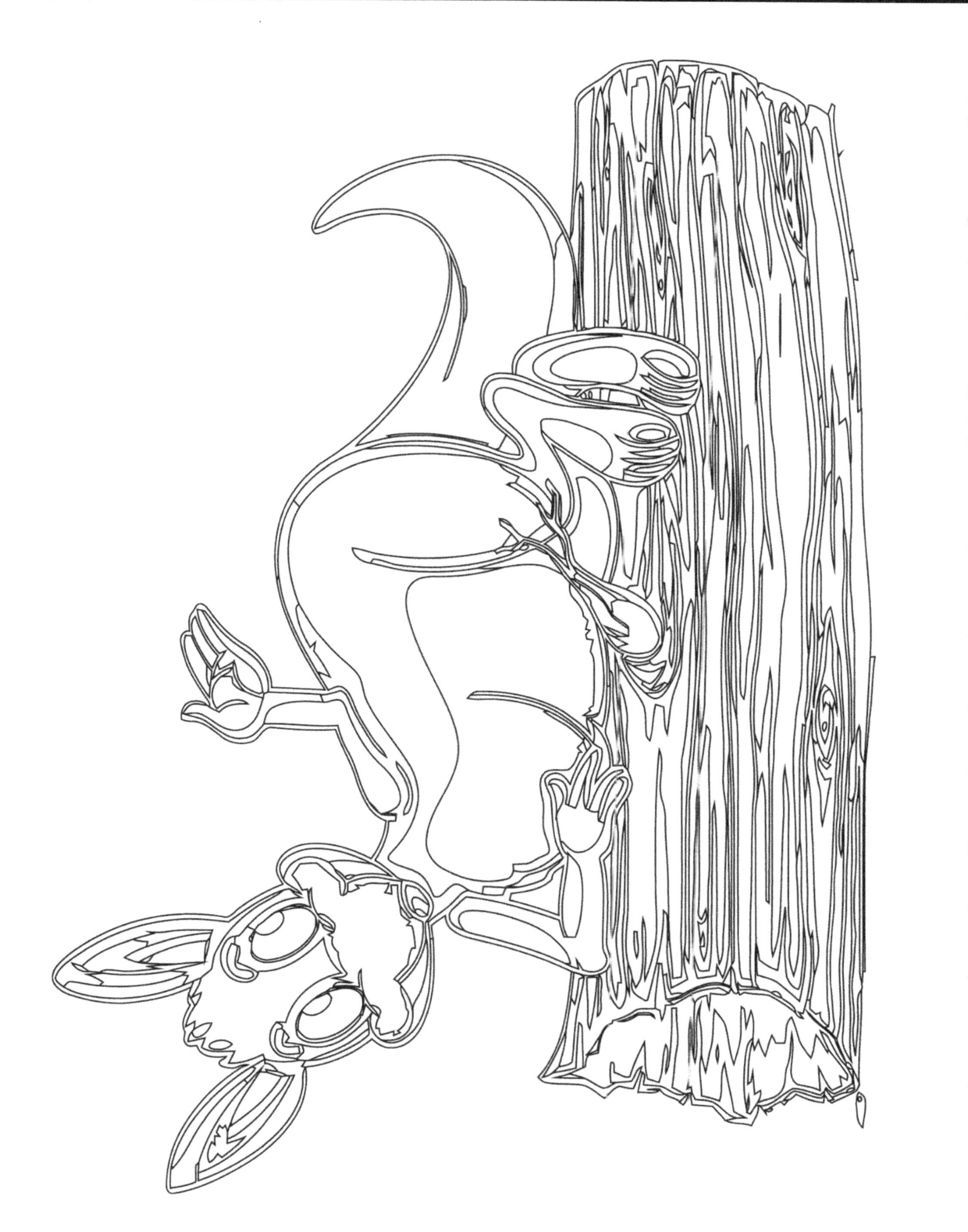

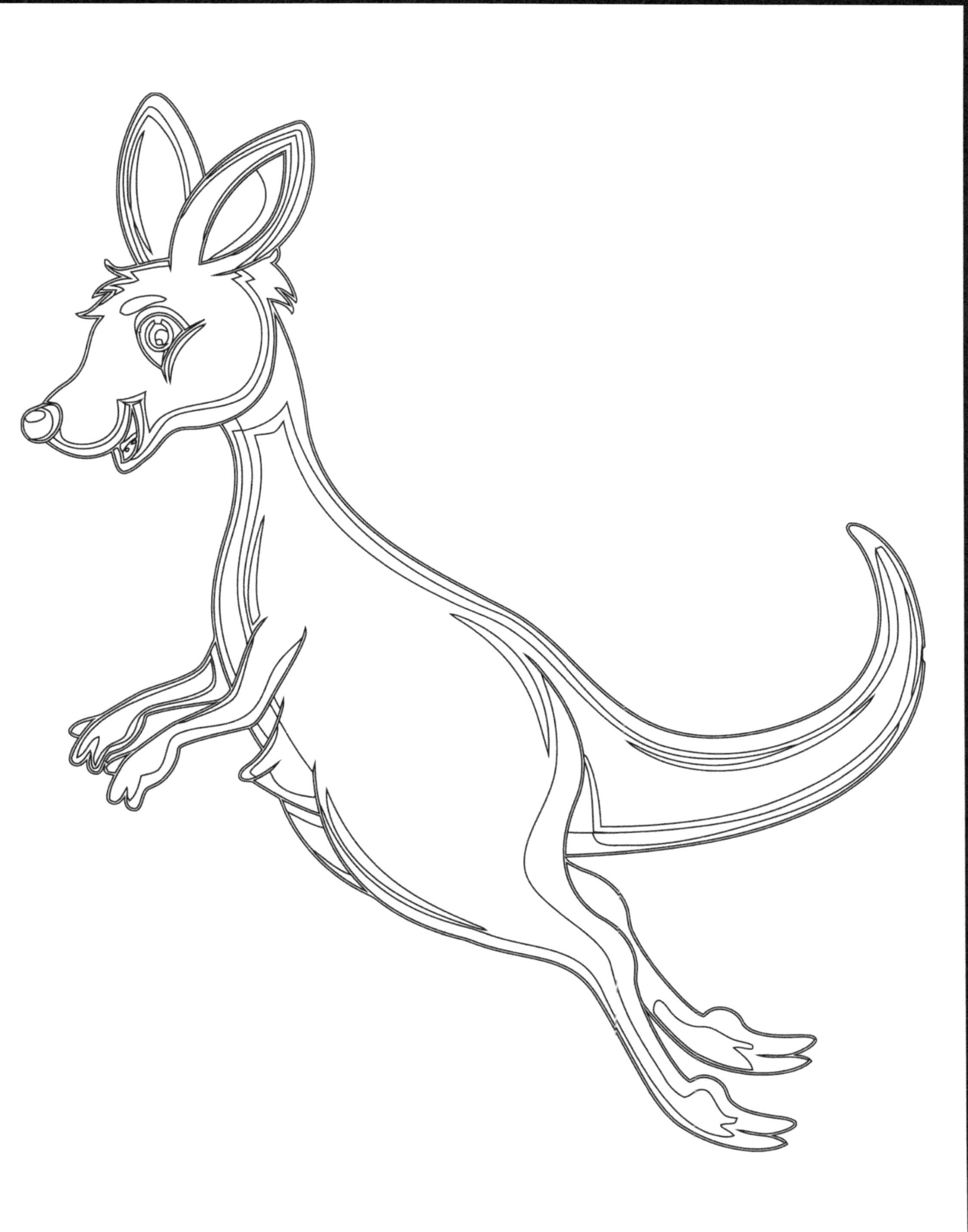

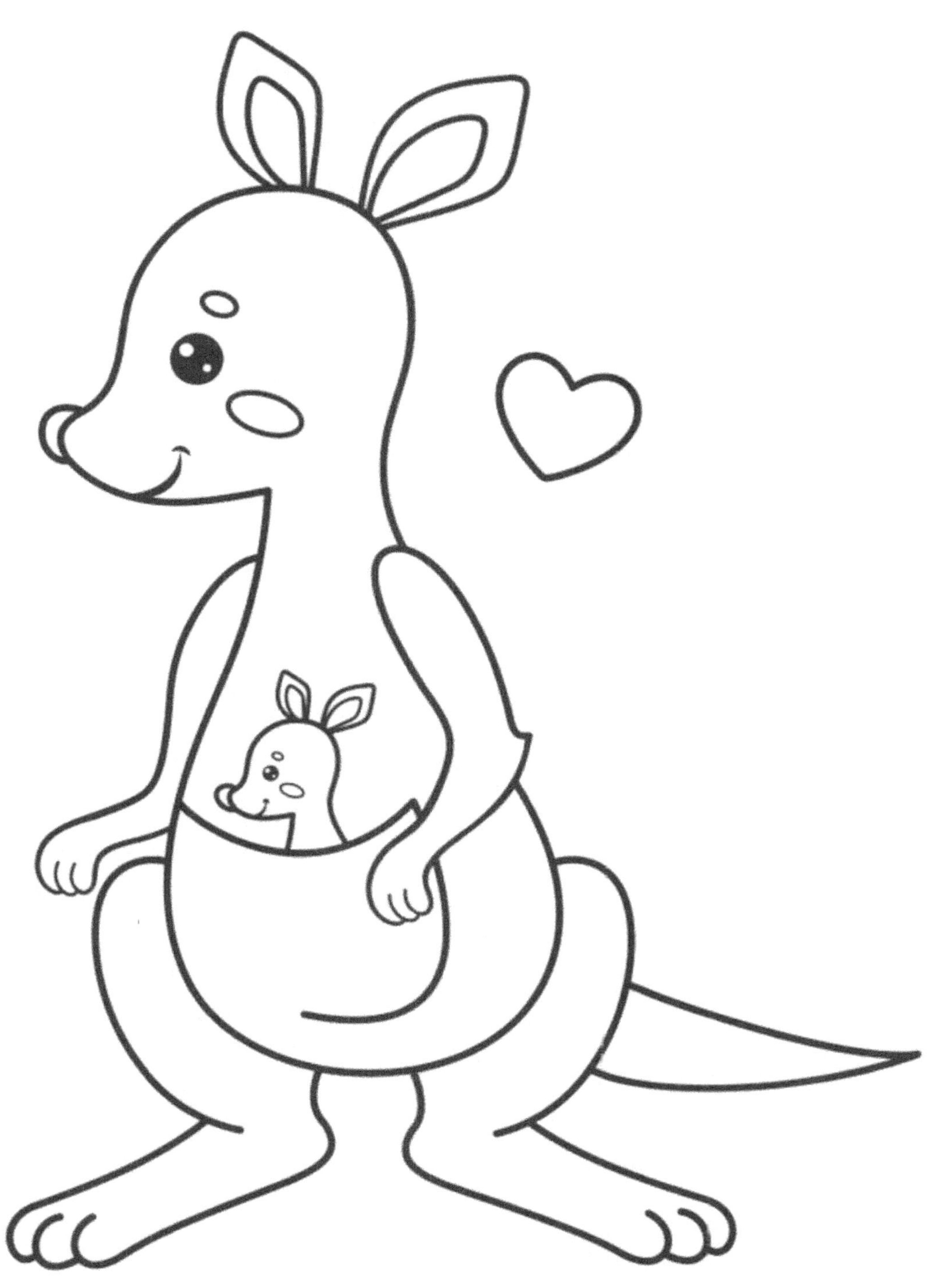

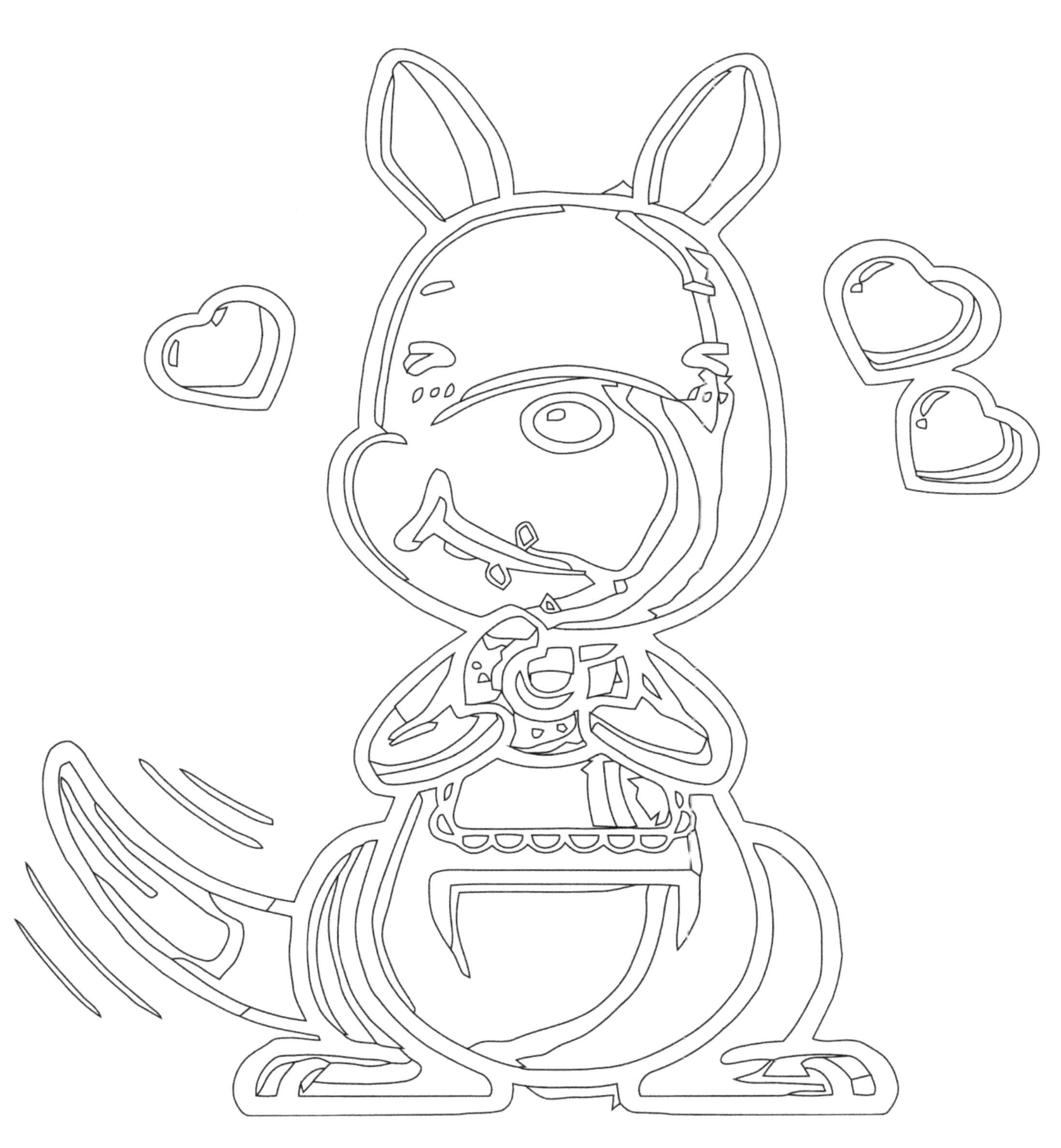

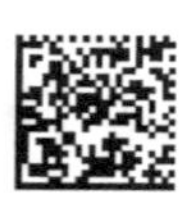